Up and Down

by Kevin Long
illustrated by Camika Walters

Practice Pre-Decodable 6

McGraw Hill Education

Bothell, WA • Chicago, IL • Columbus, OH • New York, NY

MHEonline.com

Send all inquiries to:
McGraw-Hill Education
8787 Orion Place
Columbus, OH 43240

ISBN: 978-0-02-132208-4
MHID: 0-02-132208-2

Printed in the United States of America.

8 9 10 CTM 23

The  go  .

balloons up

 go  .

People up

The  go  and .

balloons up up

 go  and  .

People up up

The  go  .

balloons down

 go 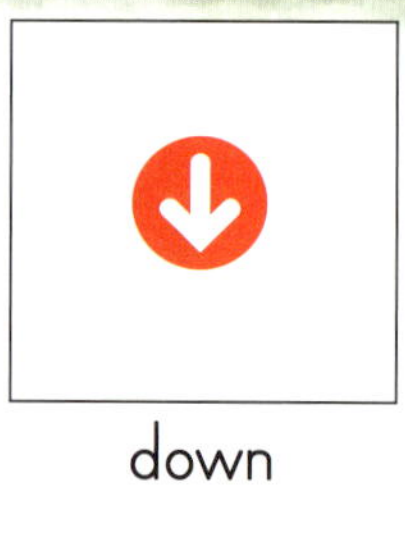.

People down